A Visit to
GERMANY

Rob Alcraft

Heinemann Library
Des Plaines, Illinois

Designed by AMR
Illustrations by Art Construction
Printed in Hong Kong/China

03 02 01 00 99
10 9 8 7 6 5 4 3 2 1

Alcraft, Rob, 1966–
    Germany / Rob Alcraft.
        p.   cm. -- (A Visit to)
    Includes bibliographical references and index.
    Summary: Introduces the land, landmarks, homes, food, clothes,
work, transportation, language, schools, recreation, and culture of
Germany.
    ISBN 1-57572-852-4
    1. Germany--Juvenile literature. 2. Germany--Social life and
customs--Juvenile literature.   [1. Germany]   I. Title.
II. Series.
DD17. A73   1999
943--dc21   99-18086
                                                                   CIP

Acknowledgments
The Publishers would like to thank the following for permission to reproduce photographs:
AKG Photo, p. 29; J. Allan Cash, pp. 10, 17, 19, 28; Robert Harding Picture Library, pp. 21, 22,
27; G. Hellier, p. 7; Larsen-Collinge, p. 13; Spectrum Color Library, p. 24; Stock Market/John
Henley, p. 25; Telegraph Color Library, pp. 6, 27; Werner Otto, pp. 5, 9, 14; Bildarchiv Huber,
p. 8; David Noton, pp. 11, 26; Josef Beck, p. 15; Antonio Mo, p. 16; Pfeiffer, p.18; Trevor
Clifford, p. 12; Trip, M. O'Brien, p. 20; M. Barlow, p. 23.

Cover photo: Britstock – IFA/Oertel

Every effort has been made to contact copyright holders of any material reproduced in this
book. Any omissions will be rectified in subsequent printings if notice is given to the Publisher.

Any words appearing in bold, **like this**, are explained in the Glossary.

Contents

Germany

Key
- Land above 3,200ft/1,000m
- Land above 1,600ft/500m
- Land above 650ft/200m
- Land above 0ft/0m/sea level
- ● Capital
- Brandenburg Gate
- Boundary

DENMARK

NORTH SEA

BALTIC SEA

NETHERLANDS

Elbe River

Berlin

North

POLAND

Cologne

G E R M A N Y

BELGIUM

Mosel River

Rhine River

CZECH REPUBLIC

FRANCE

Danube River

Munich

A L P S

AUSTRIA

SWITZERLAND

Germany is a country in the middle
of Europe. It has many big cities.

Most of the people live in cities. Germans eat, sleep, go to school, and play like you. Life in Germany is also **unique**.

Land

The land is flat and low in northern Germany. There are **marshes** and islands in the sea. The weather here is wet and mild.

There are forests, **meadows,** and mountains in southern Germany. The mountains are called the Alps. Winters here are very cold with lots of snow.

7

Landmarks

Germany's longest river is the Rhine River. Along the riverbanks are **vineyards** and beautiful castles.

This is the Brandenburg Gate. It is 200 years old. It stands in the middle of Berlin, Germany's **capital** city.

Homes

Germany's towns and cities, like Munich and Cologne, are busy places. Most people live in apartment buildings.

In the countryside there are old farm houses. They are built from wood. The buildings have wide, **sloping** roofs so the snow will slide off.

Food

Lunch is the biggest meal. There might be
a meat dish called **schnitzel** (shnit-zel)
with mashed potatoes and vegetables.

Sausage called *wurst* is a special German food. There are over 200 different kinds of sausage. Sausage can be served hot, cold, sliced, or **spicy**.

Clothes

Germans wear **modern** clothes, such as jeans and T-shirts. In winter, people wrap up in warm, thick coats and boots.

Many Germans wear special clothes for parties and festivals. Some, like this boy, might wear leather shorts called *lederhosen* and a cap with feathers.

Work

Many Germans have jobs in factories, offices, and shops. They make cars, trucks, machines, and **electrical goods**.

In the country, farmers keep cows and pigs.
They also grow grain, potatoes, and fruit.
The weather and soil are good for farming.

Transportation

Germans like to drive cars. There are many big **highways**. There are also train stations and busy airports in every city.

Ships and **barges** carry coal, steel, and oil.
They travel on Germany's rivers and
canals. Ships from the sea travel on the
Rhine River to come right into Germany.

Language

In Germany, people speak German.
Some German and English words sound
nearly the same, such as *buch* and *book*
and *haus* and *house*.

There are two ways of speaking German. One way is used when speaking with adults and important people. The other way is for friends.

School

School starts at 7:30 A.M. in Germany. There is school on Saturdays, too. Lessons always finish at lunchtime, and everyone has the afternoon off.

The children in this picture are on a school trip to the zoo. When they are in class, they learn math and German. They also learn English.

Free Time

Many Germans like to go on vacation.
In the summer families often go to the
beach. In winter when it snows, some
people go skiing in the Alps.

Many Germans enjoy sports. They join
sports clubs and play tennis and soccer.
They walk and camp in the forests and
mountains.

Celebrations

Christmas is the most important celebration in Germany. There are special markets and fairs. The streets sparkle with lights.

There is a children's festival every year
in July. Children dress up in costumes.
They parade through the streets.

The Arts

Germany is well-known for its beautiful music. The composers Beethoven and Schumann wrote music for **orchestras** and for the piano.

The story of Sleeping Beauty is a very old German **fairy tale**. It was written down by two brothers named Grimm.

Fact File

Name   The Federal Republic of Germany is the country's full name.

Capital   Germany's **capital** city is Berlin.

Language   The people speak German.

Population There are 84 million people living in Germany.

Money   German money is called marks.

Religion   Most Germans are Christians, but there are many other religions, too.

Products   Germany makes chemicals, cars, trucks, machines, and **electrical goods**.

Words You Can Learn

guten Tag (goo-ten targ)	hello
Auf Wiedersehen (owf vee-d-say-n)	goodbye
ja (ya)	yes
nein (nine)	no
danke schön (danke shern)	thank you
bitte (bitter)	please
ein (eye-n)	one
zwei (svi)	two
drei (dry)	three

Glossary

barge	Boat with a flat bottom. It can float in shallow water.
canal	River dug by people
capital	City where the government is based
electrical goods	Things like TVs and VCRs that use electricity
fairy tale	Story that involves magic and has events that could not possibly happen
highway	Big, fast road. Often a highway has three lanes of cars going each way.
marsh	Low land that is soft and wet
meadow	Grassy land
modern	New, up-to-date
orchestra	Group of people who play music using many instruments
schnitzel	Fried meat in breadcrumbs
slope	Slant, go up and down
spicy	Food with a strong, hot taste
unique	Different in a special way
vineyard	Place where grapes are grown

Index

More Books to Read

Arnold, Helen. *Postcards from Germany*. Chatham, N.J.: Raintree Steck-Vaughn, 1995.

Dahl, Michael. *Germany*. Danbury, Conn.: Children's Press, 1997. An older reader can help you with this book.

Haskins, Jim. *Count Your Way Through Germany*. Minneapolis, Minn.: Lerner Publishing Group, 1992.